KU-175-301

POCKET SERIES

# Buses & Trams

By Henry Hirst

Daily Mirror
HOPE
HOPE
FTE 630B

# Contents

**▪ POCKET SERIES ▪**


First published in the UK in 2010
By Instinctive Product Development





Publishers: Vanessa Gardner and Carl Edwards

Printed and bound in China

ISBN: 978-1-907657-31-3

Designed by: BrainWave

Creative Director: Kevin Gardner

Written by Henry Hirst

Images courtesy of Mirrorpix and Shutterstock

COUNTY FIRE OFFICE
Johnnie Walker
GENERAL
PARIPAN

# Introduction

It is now 150 years since the first recognised public transport was provided on the streets of Britain's towns and cities; over the years since then, there have been many changes to the scale and nature of urban public transport but its fundamental raison d'être – to move large numbers of people from home to shop, to school and to work efficiently and cheaply – remains unchanged.

Since the opening of the first tramway, in 1860, the streets of Britain have witnessed a great variety of types of vehicle and there remains considerable nostalgia for many of these models. The end of electric tramway operation in many towns and cities was witnessed by countless thousands marking the loss of a familiar and much-loved mode of transport whilst, more recently, the final withdrawal of the Routemaster – widely regarded as one of the greatest designs

■ **LEFT:** Steet scene showing the traffic in Picadilly Circus, Central London. Circa 1925.

■ **ABOVE:** A line-up of buses with, nearest the camera, two Routemasters.

produced in Britain since the end of World War 2 – was also marked by large crowds in the streets witnessing history in the making.

In many respects the history of public transport over a century-and-a-half is also a history of urban Britain, the evolution of the High Street, with its familiar shop fascias, the impact of two world wars and the growth of the private motorcar and the road haulage industry. Photographs taken of trams in the early 20th century show how much – and in many cases – how little has changed over the past century. Although the shop names in town and city centres may have changed or been modified, the buildings behind the facades and much of the street furniture remain unchanged.

In *Buses & Trams* the reader is taken back through the past 150 years to explore the history of public transport in urban Britain and how it has helped to shape our view of the landscape in towns and cities nationwide.

■ **TOP INSET:** Northumberland Street in Newcastle. 1938.

■ **ABOVE INSET:** Old High Street in Newport, Wales, circa 1900.

■ **ABOVE:** Steam tram in Birmingham, 1882.

# Historical Overview

The 19th century witnessed one of the great social revolutions when, as a result of the Industrial Revolution and the concentration of workers in factories, towns and cities expanded rapidly. As these urban communities grew, so too did the needs of the population to be able to move around them. Transport was increasingly needed to allow workers to commute from home to place of work and, in an era when the town and city centre grew as commercial centres, good connections were needed between suburbs and the main centre. For much of the 19th century the horse remained the primary form of urban transport but there were severe limits as to what the horse could achieve on the poor roads of the country.

The first phase of the transport revolution occurred in 1860 with the opening of the first street tramway in the British Isles – indeed the first in Europe – in Birkenhead. Promoted by an American émigré, George Francis Train, this tramway and one that had opened the following year in London, drawing upon technology developed in the USA, were to be the first of many horse-operated tramways that emerged during the next decade. Such was the rate of progress that a new law – the Tramways Act – was passed in 1870; this law governed the way in which tramways were authorised and constructed. Amongst the provisions was the clause that made the tramway operator responsible for the maintenance of a section of the road stretching 18 inches on either side of the track. Inevitably, at a time when the roads were generally not well maintained, this led to other road users seeking to use this well-maintained section of road.

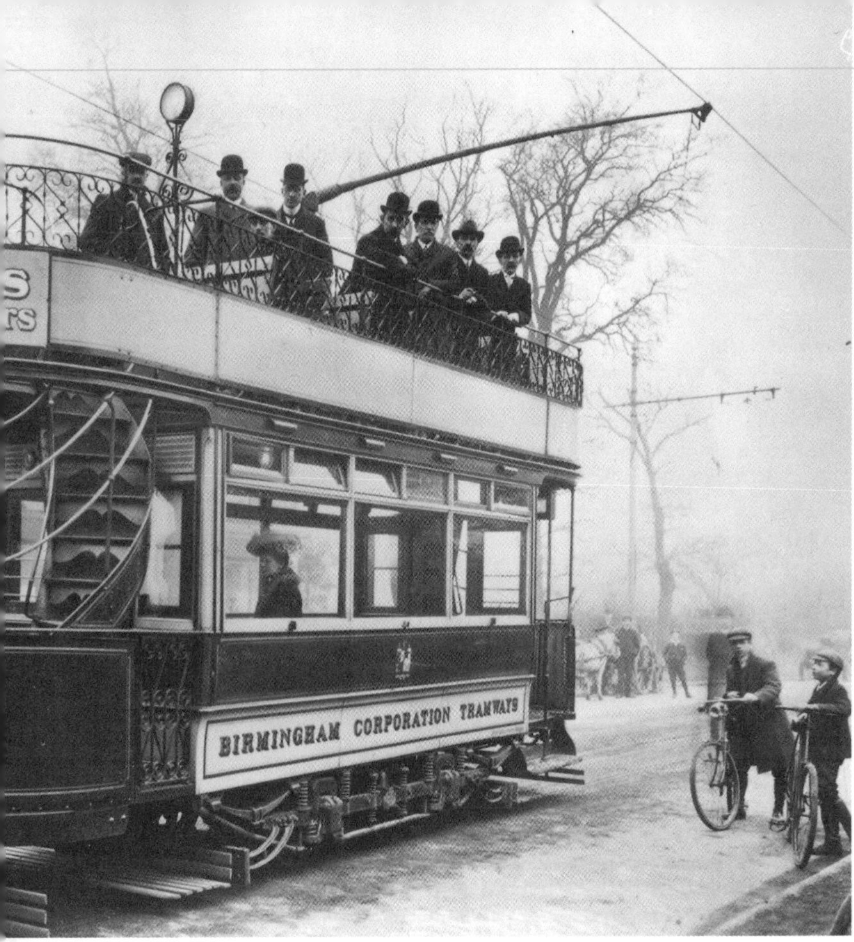


■ **ABOVE:** The first electric-powered tram in Erdington, Birmingham, 1907.

Horse-operated tramways were built through much of Britain and many survived into the early 20th century – indeed one still operates in Douglas on the Isle of Man – but the technology was obsolete almost from the dawn of the tramway age as steam engines were easily designed to operate in the road. The first successful carriage of fare-paying passengers using steam traction on a tramway was in West Bromwich in 1876 and, like the horse tram before it, the number of steam-tram operators soon grew.

One of the earlier steam-tram operators was Huddersfield in 1883; this town was, however, unusual in that it represented the first occasion on which public transport was provided by the local municipality. Historically, tramway operators had been company-owned, albeit with track often leased by the local authority and with parliamentary acts that allowed the local authority to take over operations after a given period (usually seven years). Huddersfield, however, had been unable to find a company willing to take its lease on and so had to take on the operation itself; ultimately, most major towns and cities in Britain were to see their buses and trams operated by municipally-owned fleets. The largest exception, which retained company-operated vehicles throughout, was Bristol.

Steam traction enabled larger trams to operate but was dirty and noisy and an alternative form of traction was soon to be made available – electricity. By the early 1880s experiments in electric traction had proved its practicality and the first lines to be electrically-operated opened. In mainland Britain, the first conduit-operated tramway – Blackpool – opened in 1885 and, subsequently converted to overhead operation, this seaside resort was the one first-generation street tramway to survive through to the 21st century. Overhead electrification first made its appearance in Leeds in 1891 following a successful experiment in Edinburgh the previous year. From now,

■ **ABOVE:** A Blackpool tram.

■ **ABOVE:** A preserved 'B'-type bus with Chelsea Pensioners on board the open-top double-deck bus.

through to the outbreak of World War 1, there was to be a massive explosion in the number of tramways built in the country, stretching from Cruden Bay in the extreme northeast of Scotland to Camborne in Cornwall and from Dover in Kent to Rothesay in Scotland. There were also numerous tramways in Ireland plus others on the Isle of Man and the Channel Islands. No self-respecting town or city could afford to be without its tramway.

However, even as the electric tramcar was under massive expansion, the seeds of its destruction were already becoming evident. The costs of construction and maintenance were high and as the urban areas continued to expand, alternative and cheaper forms of transport were required.

Two rubber-tyred vehicles came to pose a threat to the tram: the petrol or diesel-powered bus and the electrically-powered trolleybus. The internal combustion engine, developed from the late 19th century enabled vehicles to be built that could operate without the massive investment required in the construction of tramways. The first petrol-drive buses to appear started operation in the early 20th century and, in 1903, Eastbourne became the first municipal operator of these vehicles. This was a significant move because Eastbourne had never constructed a tramway and thus the bus became its first foray into the provision of public transport. Where Eastbourne led, other operators soon followed, many using the relatively inefficient and small vehicles of the day to act as 'feeders' into the tram network. But as the motorbus grew more efficient so its ability to compete with the tram came into sharp focus.

The trolleybus offered a halfway house between the tram and the bus; powered by electricity, it required the overhead supply network of the tram but not the investment that the tram required in track. Following experiments in London and Hove, the first two systems opened simultaneously in Bradford and Leeds in June 1911. Never as popular as the tram, there were less than 50 operators of trolleybuses in the British Isles many lasting for only a relatively short period. Although London at one time possessed the largest trolleybus network in the world, the entire system was scrapped by May 1962. The final surviving network, the pioneering system of Bradford, was to last a decade longer before finally succumbing in March 1972. Today, it is still possible to ride on a trolleybus but only on a preserved example at one of three museums nationwide – Black Country, Carlton Colville and Sandtoft – that operate them.

It was World War 1 that was to lead to one of the major developments in the industry. While the tram remained dominant through the wartime years – although the first electric tramway to close, Sheerness, did disappear during the war – the arrival of peace brought several thousand ex-army lorries on to the market and countless returning servicemen capable of driving them. Many of these lorries were converted into basic buses and coaches and, in an era before any form of regulation, were launched into public service, often in competition with the existing tram or trolleybus operators.

For the tram, the early 1920s were a turning point. For many small systems, coming to the end of the useful life of their first tramcars, the costs of replacement were prohibitive particularly in an era when petrol-engined buses were relatively cheap and even some major operators were starting to experiment. In Birmingham, in 1922, the Nechells route was converted from tram to trolleybus operation, the first of many that would succumb over the next 30 years. Between 1920 and 1930 almost 30 tramway systems were abandoned; some were relatively small (like Burton & Ashby) but others (like Wolverhampton) represented systems in large towns. During the 1930s, this process was to

■ **ABOVE:** Wives of tramway men acting as conductors while the men are away fighting, 1914.

■ **ABOVE:** A bottle neck is created at a junction in Birmingham whilst the points are changed for a tram.

accelerate: in 1930 alone 15 tramway networks were converted to either bus or trolleybus operation.

During the 1920s the authorities became increasingly conscious that the competition engendered by the post-World War 1 operators was not sensible, particularly in an environment where the economy had struggled to regain prosperity. As a result, the Road Traffic Act of 1930 was brought in. Amongst its various provisions was the regulation of bus and coach services; for the next 50 years, this was to be the guiding act for the provision of public transport. It was only following the Transport Act of 1985, which brought in deregulation, that the powers of the 1930 Act to determine public transport services were finally largely abolished outside Greater London.

Another piece of important legislation followed shortly after the 1930 Act; this was the creation of the London Passenger Transport Board (LPTB). Created as a result of the London Passenger Transport Act of 1933, the LPTB came formally into existence on 1 July 1933. Incorporating all public transport – trams, buses, trolleybuses and underground lines – within the Metropolis, the LPTB – commonly abbreviated to London Transport – provided a central control and co-ordination for the provision of public transport throughout the Greater London area. Under the LPTB's auspices, the capital's small trolleybus network, inherited from London United Tramways, was rapidly extended and much investment went into the development of the underground network. The LPTB became the London Transport Executive on 1 January 1948; following nationalisation as a subsidiary of the British Transport Commission it became the London Transport Board on 1 January 1963, the London Transport Executive on 1 January 1970, London Regional Transport on 29 June 1984 and, finally, Transport for London (TfL) on 2 July 2000. Although the name and some of the responsibilities may have changed – TfL, for example, no longer owns the buses that operate the routes that it franchises – the basic function of providing co-ordinated public transport for London remains largely unchanged.

Although the 1930s were to witness an almost inexorable decline in the number of British tramways, there were many – such as Blackpool, Edinburgh, Glasgow, Leeds and Liverpool – that continued to invest in new vehicles and routes and there were still some 50 tramway operations in Britain at the outbreak of war in September 1939. Inevitably the wartime years, with the pressure to mount total war, put strain on the public transport industry. Buses and tramways suffered severe damage from German air-raids; most notably the assault on Coventry in November 1940 which resulted in the abandonment of the city's tramway network, one of a handful of tramways to be converted to bus or tram operation during the war;

**ABOVE:** Mechanics checking the engine of a Leyland bus in 1957.

another was Bristol where the elderly open-top fleet was replaced by buses in 1941 following a Luftwaffe raid that demolished the city's power station. Another consequence of war was that there was a dearth of capacity for the production of new vehicles; a handful of manufacturers were permitted to produce buses and trolleybuses, but these were produced for the most part to wartime 'utility' standards and many were quickly rebodied once peace was restored to extend their operational lives.

With peace in 1945 came further change. The new Labour government nationalised the LPTB and the bus interests of the Tilling Group, which both became subsidiaries of the new established British Transport Commission. With peace restored, the decline in the number of British tramways continued, with operators such as Hull, Leicester, Manchester and Southampton all succumbing. The decade was also to witness the last new trolleybus system

711

in the country, with the opening of the Glasgow system in 1949. Elsewhere there continued to be limited investment in some of the surviving tramway networks including Aberdeen, Edinburgh, Glasgow, Leeds and Sheffield, with routes extended and new vehicles delivered.

The next decade was, however, to see the industry swing almost exclusively towards the diesel bus as the only form of local transport. Tramway systems throughout the country disappeared; these included Cardiff (1950), London (1952), Birmingham (1953), Belfast (1954), Dundee (1956) and Liverpool (1957). Even those systems that had modernised were to succumb: Edinburgh (1956), Aberdeen (1958), Leeds (1959), Sheffield (1960) and Glasgow (1962). By the end of the process, there remained one conventional tramway in the British Isles outside the Isle of Man – Blackpool – and even here the system had shrunk considerably over the previous decade. For the trolleybus, the prognosis was equally dire, although the major conversions did not occur until the 1960s – for example London (1962), Manchester (1966), Glasgow (1967), Huddersfield (1968), Belfast (1968) and Cardiff (1970) – with the last, Bradford, succumbing in 1972.

With the all-conquering bus came further changes to the organisation of the industry. In 1963 the Scottish Bus Group was established; it controlled the nationalised bus industry north of the border. In England and Wales, the bus interests of the British Electric Traction (BET) were nationalised to form, in 1969, the new National Bus Company (NBC) alongside the ex-Tilling Group companies. A number of the major independent operators, such as West Riding, also sold out to NBC. More radical change was to come in the big metropolitan areas outside London. Merseyside, Greater Manchester, Tyne & Wear, West Midlands, South Yorkshire, West Yorkshire and Strathclyde Passenger Transport Executives (PTEs)

**LEFT:** A Blackpool tram.

took over the control and co-ordination of public transport in their areas between 1969 and 1975. This resulted in the disappearance of many of the historic municipal fleets; West Yorkshire PTE, for example, incorporated the fleets of Bradford, Halifax, Huddersfield and Leeds. Co-ordination with local NBC operators saw the disappearance of many traditional operators; North Western Road Car, for example, disappeared when its routes and vehicles within Greater Manchester were taken over by the PTE with the remainder passing to other NBC operators.

The next major change came with the Conservative government of the 1980s. Two policies – Deregulation and Privatisation – came to change forever the traditional face of the public transport industry. Deregulation was one of the consequences of the Transport Act of 1985; it meant that, outside London, competition was permitted on all commercially-registered routes and that, for those routes for which there was no commercial operator, local authorities could provide a subsidy. Initially, Deregulation meant the streets of some of the country's biggest cities became clogged with large numbers of additional vehicles as new operators entered the fray. 'Bus wars' broke out and, in many cases, smaller and weaker operators were forced out of the market. With this, and the onset of privatisation (which resulted in the sale of all of the state-owned operators and many of the surviving municipals), the new super-groups grew up; today, much of the bus industry is dominated by four major operators – Arriva, First Group, Go-Ahead and Stagecoach – whose vehicles are now a familiar sight throughout the country.

The last decade of the 20th century saw a further major shift in public transport; at the start of the 1960s, the tram was consigned to the history books in Britain. Throughout Europe, however, and much of the world, tramways continued to prosper and, from the late 1980s, interest

■ **ABOVE:** The army driving and conducting on the buses during the bus strike, 1944.

in the creation of second-generation tramways grew in the UK. Although the first – Tyne & Wear Metro – opened originally in 1980, this was very much a conversion of the existing British Rail suburban network. For street running, Britain had to wait for Manchester Metrolink (first section opened 1992), Sheffield Supertram (1994), Midland Metro (1999), Croydon Tramlink (2000) and Nottingham Express Transit (2004). With these new systems, it is possible to see modern single-deck trams operating in British streets and further projects, such as Edinburgh and extensions to existing systems, are already either under construction or planned. Moreover, with the recently approved project for Leeds, it looks as though the trolleybus may also return to Britain. As environmental concerns increase, the role of public transport in the urban environment becomes ever more significant; 150 years on, the tram and the bus seem once again to be central to life in towns and cities.

■ **RIGHT:** Crowds turned out to see the last tram through Birmingham City Centre in 1953.

CARS LOAD HERE
FOR
ERDINGTON
2
NO ENTRY
2
THE END

■ **ABOVE:** A Clydebank tram, the last to run in Glasgow.

■ **ABOVE:** Last journey of the London trolleybus, 1962.

**ABOVE:** Fintona horse tram.

# Evolution of Buses and Trams

The first tramcars to operate in the British Isles at Birkenhead were small. Although the initial vehicles were imported, a factory, Starbucks, was soon opened in Birkenhead, and this was to supply a significant number of trams for both the domestic and European markets. Horse trams, constructed as both single- and double-deckers, were generally relatively small and light, relying as they did upon a single horse or pair of horses for power. Although single-deck trams were normally fully enclosed, with the exception of the platform vestibules, the upper decks were open to the elements.

Tramcar design progressed with the

arrival of the steam tram. The engine was normally a small four-wheel design, with wheels and motion hidden in order to protect other road users, but the power that steam offered over and above the horse meant that steam-tram trailers could be significantly larger than the earlier horse-tram trailers and some bogie trailers with large capacities were constructed. One of the problems for steam-tram passengers, particularly those on the upper deck, was the smoke and steam that emanated from the engine; in order to counter this, double-deck trailers started to appear with rudimentary top covers. These normally covered the seating area alone, leaving the balconies and the staircases still open to the wind and rain.

The early electric trams, developed from the mid-1880s onwards, saw mainly a return to the more modest open-top four-wheel designs that had characterised the era of the horse tram. However, it was not long before the electric tramcar

gradually evolved. Top covers, lower-deck vestibules and enclosed top-deck balconies were soon to make their appearance but not all systems were to modernise. Bristol, for example, where the company-operated network was regularly perceived to be under the threat of municipalisation – a seven-year clause allowing local authorities to take over company-operated lines was a feature of tramway legislation – meant that the city's trams remained unmodernised right through until final closure in

■ **ABOVE:** Steam tram engine at Parnell Place, Newcastle.

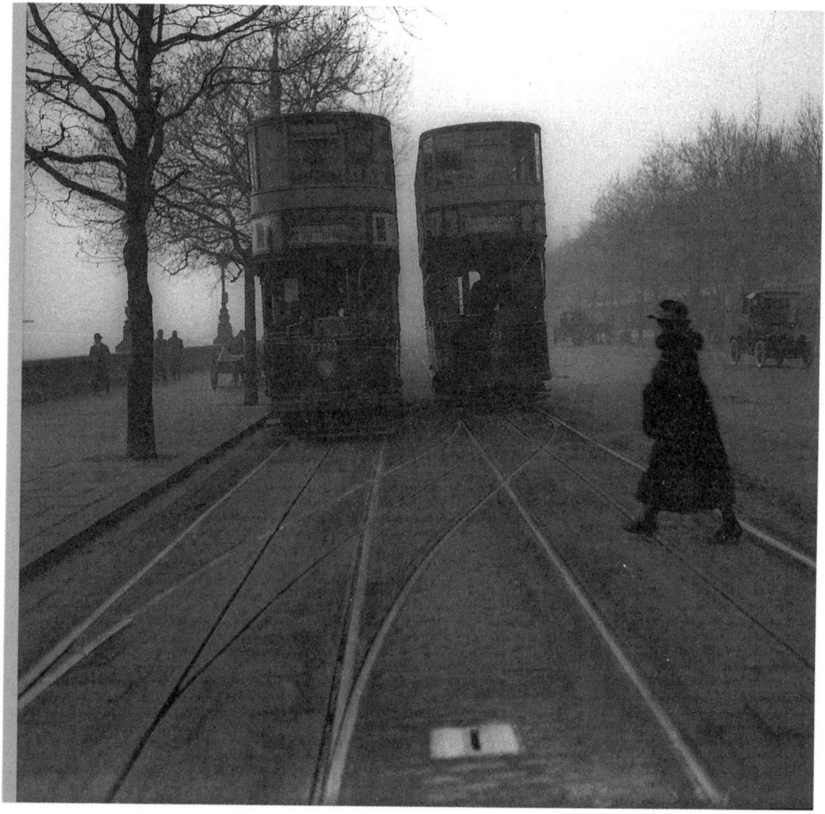

■ **ABOVE:** Tramcars on the Embankment, circa 1915.

■ **ABOVE:** The last tram to run in London.

1941. Other factors that prevented the complete modernisation of tram fleets were restrictions placed on a number of narrow-gauge operators, particularly in hilly areas. Although most of the important tram operators selected the standard gauge – 4ft 8.5in (1.5m) – as used on the railway network, there were a number that adopted other gauges. In the West Midlands, for example, Birmingham and other operators selected 3ft 6in (1.1m), a gauge that was shared by Halifax in the West Riding of Yorkshire. Neighbouring Bradford adopted the 4ft 0in (1.2m) gauge, however, but both Bradford and Halifax were barred from operating fully-enclosed double-deck trams as a result of the steep routes over which some of their trams operated.

For many tramway operators the original tramcar fleet, albeit modernised over time in most cases, was to suffice through to closure; by the 1920s and 1930s, however, a number of systems were starting to modernise their fleets with updated vehicles. Blackpool, for instance, was to see streamlined double- and single-deck trams constructed in large numbers during the 1930s; many of these, maintained and upgraded, were to survive for some 60 years or more, becoming a familiar sight to visitors to the town. It was only with the decision to upgrade the coastal tramway towards the end of the first decade of the 21st century that the surviving veterans were to be gradually withdrawn. Cities like Glasgow, with the 'Coronation' class bogie cars, and Liverpool, with the 'Green Goddess' bogie cars and the 'Baby Grand' four-wheelers, invested heavily in modern trams.

Post-war, although tramways were gradually to be eliminated from the streets of Britain, modern trams continued to be produced. In Blackpool, for example, the 'Coronation' class of single-deck trams was delivered in the early 1950s, whilst Glasgow invested in the 'Cunarder' class of double-deck trams and Sheffield in a batch of stylish four-wheel double-deck trams produced by Roberts of Wakefield. Most startling of all, Leeds built or converted three single-deck trams – Nos 600-602 – that were amongst the most modern in Europe at the time with the intention that these vehicles would form the precursor of a fleet designed to permit the construction of tramway subways. In reality, however, these post-war trams were too little too late; the writing was on the wall for tramway operators and most of the vehicles constructed were destined to have very short lives.

From the late 1980s onwards and with the development of the second-generation tramways in places like Sheffield and Croydon, continental-style single-deck articulated trams have become the norm and this process will undoubtedly continue as further new systems, such as Edinburgh and the modernised coastal tramway at Blackpool, are completed.

Although an early experimental trolleybus had been an open-top double-decker, the first trolleybuses

■ **TOP:** Sheffield Supertram. ■ **ABOVE:** A Liverpool Green Goddess tram.

introduced to public service in Leeds and Bradford in 1911 had been small single-deckers. It was a decade before double-deck trolleybuses first appeared in significant numbers and, from the mid-1920s, trolleybus body design was to show remarkably little variation until the final UK trolleybuses were built in the early 1960s. The vast majority were two- or three-axle double-deckers with full-fronted bodywork and rear open platforms. There were exceptions; Notts & Derby, a company operator in the Midlands, had trolleybuses bodied in a style similar to contemporary buses with a half-cab and fake cowling over a non-existent engine whilst later front-entrance bodywork with power-operated doors appeared in limited numbers. As with buses, trolleybus design resulted in longer and wider vehicles as restrictions on size were relaxed. Amongst the largest was a batch of 35ft-long (10.7m) single-deckers supplied to Glasgow with Burlingham bodywork but these 10 vehicles were destined to have a working life of less than a decade.

Buses, like trams, started as horse drawn and there were distinct similarities between the scale of the two. It was only after the invention of the internal combustion engine, pioneered by two Germans – Gottlieb Daimler and Karl Benz – in the late 19th century that the first powered buses emerged. Early buses were manufactured by a large number of companies – some were later to become dominant like Daimler whilst others like Gilford and Maudslay were to be relatively short-lived. A number of early manufacturers used commercial vehicle chassis types as the basis for entering the bus market. Early double-deck models again tended to be open-top and fitted with open staircases; the driver also had little protection with the centrally-placed cab being open to the elements. The classic type of bus from this early era is the London 'B' type of which several thousand were produced and of which many were

■ **ABOVE LEFT:** Gottlieb Daimler. ■ **ABOVE:** Karl Benz.

■ **ABOVE:** An early double-deck bus.

shipped to France during World War 1 to help move the troops behind the frontline. Early touring coaches – or charabancs – were also built; these were single-deck and again often open-top (although normally fitted with removable roofs in case of inclement weather.

The major boom in the bus industry came in the years immediately after World War 1 when the unregulated environment and the availability of large numbers of military-surplus vehicles meant that it was relatively easy to start out in the bus and coach industry. Towards the end of the 1920s – with G. J. Rackham at AEC at the forefront following a four-year sojourn in the USA – British bus design can be said to have developed the classic rear-entrance front-engined single- and double-deck model that was to dominate production through to the development of the rear- and underfloor-engined models from the late 1950s onwards. With the AEC Regent and the Leyland Titan double-deck models and the AEC Regal and Leyland Tiger single-deck models for example, vehicles capable of replacing trams and trolleybuses had been developed. Although the early models were petrol-engined, by the early 1930s, diesel – or oil as it was known at the time – engines were under production and became the preferred choice for most operators.

From this era came the standard bus dimensions – length of 27ft 6in (8.4m)

**ABOVE:** Leyland Titan bus in the old Glasgow Corporation livery.

**RIGHT:** An AEC Regent bus.

19
STREATHAM COMMON
ANGEL ISLINGTON ROSEBERY Ave
PICCADILLY CIRCUS
HYDE PARK CORNER
SLOANE St KINGS Rd
BATTERSEA Bdg Rd TRINITY Rd
EVERY
WEDNESDAY
CTURE
OST
CROSSE & BLACKWELL
BRANSTON PICKLE
54
EGO 426

■ **ABOVE:** An articulated London bus passes one nearly 50 years its senior.

and a width of 7ft 6in (2.3m) – but these restrictions were gradually relaxed so that vehicles eventually became 8ft (2.4m) in width and progressively lengthened to 30ft (9.1m), 33ft (10.1m) and ultimately to 36ft (11m) in length. Recent developments have seen the size of buses extended yet further with three-axle vehicles of 39ft 4in (12m) now in operation; the maximum permitted length of a double-deck vehicle in Britain is now 49ft 3in (15m). Articulated buses were illegal in the UK until 1980 but until the recent – and unpopular – introduction of this type of vehicle to London, relatively few have operated in the UK. Articulated buses in the UK are up to 60ft (18m) in length, much longer than the maximum permitted for conventional single-deck vehicles of 46ft (14m). Over the years, vehicles have got larger as a means of increasing passenger capacity – both sitting and standing – and of improving the financial position of the bus industry.

Traditionally double-deck bus bodies had been supplied as either 'highbridge' or 'lowbridge' versions; the latter was designed to permit the operation of double-deck buses on routes where low bridges were a problem. In order to provide sufficient headroom for the upper deck, the seats were offset and accessed by a sunken aisle to one side. This had the effect of reducing the headroom above some of the seats on the lower deck. The first double-deck design that succeeded in providing sufficient headroom on both decks but with a lower overall height was the Bristol Lodekka, launched in 1949. As a result of the restrictions imposed on the supply of Bristol vehicles to non-Tilling Group companies, the model was licensed to Dennis – as the Dennis Loline – for other operators. Other manufacturers followed suit with AEC producing the Bridgemaster and Albion, a subsidiary of Leyland, manufacturing the Lowlander.

Although the front-engined bus was originally produced largely with the open rear platform, so familiar from the Routemaster, increasingly operators decided to move the entrance to the front and fit doors. Later versions of the Lodekka, the Leyland PD, AEC Regent V and Daimler CVG6 were all so fitted; this improvement helped to improve safety and also aided passenger comfort.

The next major development in bus design came with the construction of the rear-engined double-deck Leyland Atlantean in 1958. The result of the transfer of the engine to the rear of the vehicle allowed the passenger entrance to be moved forward and thus opened the way to the one-person operation (OPO). In an era when labour costs were becoming an increasing strain on the bus industry and when passenger levels were in decline, the loss of the conductor made considerable economic sense. The Atlantean was to be followed by the Daimler Fleetline and by the Bristol VR. Guy attempted a radical solution to the front-engined model – the Wulfrunian

■ **ABOVE:** A conductor looks out from the platform of his Routemaster bus during the London Smogs of 1962.

– but this was not a commercial success. The final death knell for the traditional front-engined double-deck bus came with the alternation to the grants given to assist the purchase of new buses. Towards the end of the 1960s, the decision was made that in future, grants would only be given for double-deckers that were designed for OPO. Production of the final front-engined double-deck models ceased in the early 1970s.

The same shift to OPO single-deckers also occurred in the 1960s with models such as the AEC Swift, the Bristol RE and the Leyland Panther. Daimler's Fleetline was also made available as a single-decker, although not supplied in large numbers.

Following the end of production of the Routemaster – the last double-deck design to be produced in co-operation between London Transport and AEC – the standard London double-deck bus – the DM/DMS series of rear-engined vehicles – was effectively the Daimler Fleetline; several thousand of these were delivered. Since production of the DMS ceased, London Transport, particularly since the privatisation of the operating companies, has acquired a range of vehicles. The most controversial of these are undoubtedly the Mercedes-built articulated single-deckers introduced some five years ago. Many of these were acquired as part of the programme to replace the final Routemasters in service but such is their unpopularity that they are already being phased out in favour of new double-deck models. The Mayor of London, Boris Johnson, was elected partly on the policy of getting a Routemaster for the 21st century designed and built; this process is currently underway although the final design has yet to be agreed.

Today, the bus is very different in size and design from those that appeared at the dawn of the 20th century but the basic principle of carrying sizeable numbers of passengers remains unchanged.

■ **ABOVE:** Mayor of London, Boris Johnson, with his waxwork model at Madame Tussauds, 2009.

# Manufacturers

## AEC

The Associated Equipment Company – better known as AEC – was the principal supplier of buses to London Transport for some 60 years. The company was established in 1912 as a subsidiary of the Underground group of companies, a grouping that included the London General Omnibus Company (LGOC). LGOC operated the majority of the bus services in London prior to the creation of the London Passenger Transport Board in 1933 and had started to manufacture its own buses in 1909. AEC, based at Walthamstow initially and at Southall from 1929, produced buses, trucks (from 1916) and also trolleybuses for a brief period (1931-38). The company's first buses, a design that it inherited from the LGOC, was the 'B'-type, of which some 2,500 were constructed by 1913; many of these were to be shipped to France during World War 1 for use in moving troops. During the 1920s and 1930s, AEC was at the forefront of British bus design and development, with much of its production destined for London but the company also had considerable success in selling to municipal operators throughout the country as well as to constituent companies within the BET Group. Classic designs of the pre-World War 2 period included the AEC Regent, the three-axle Renown, and the single-deck Regal, all of which first appeared in 1929. The Regent was to form the basis of the pre-war London Transport 'RT'-type. The company expanded post-World War 2 with the acquisition of Crossley and Maudslay in 1948 and changed the name of the holding company to Associated

Commercial Vehicles (ACV). In 1961 a further well-known manufacturer – Thornycroft of Basingstoke – was acquired. However, this was to be followed in 1962 by the sale of ACV to Leyland. Initially, AEC was retained as a separate brand, with production of the Regent V, Routemaster and other models continuing but with the rationalisation of the British bus industry in the 1970s, Leyland was to close the Southall factory in 1979. By this date, production at Southall was exclusively single-deck with models such as the Reliance and Merlin, the latter primarily for London Transport, being manufactured.

■ **ABOVE:** Various preserved AEC Routemasters at the 2008 Alton bus rally at Anstey Park.

■ **ABOVE:** A line-up of Bristol buses including examples of VRs and LHs.

## Bristol

Another major builder whose origins lay with an operator, Bristol Commercial Vehicles (BCV) began as the bus-building division of the Bristol Tramways & Carriage Company (BTCC). In 1908 the operator manufactured its first buses at its Filton depot; five years later, production moved to a purpose-built factory at Brislington, which was to be the company's base until closure in 1983. In 1931 BTCC was taken over by the Tilling Group, a company that owned bus interests through much of the country, and in 1948 the Tilling Group itself became nationalised and part of the British Transport Commission. Ownership by Tilling Group meant that Bristol-built buses became the preferred vehicles for other group companies and, after nationalisation, there were severe restrictions on the supply of Bristol buses beyond the ex-Tilling Group companies. This restriction applied until 1965 when the Leyland Motor Corporation acquired a 25% stake in the Transport Holding Company (THC). In 1955, the bus-manufacturing business was separated from BTCC to become BCV, which was to become a subsidiary of the THC in 1963. Following the creation of the National Bus Company in 1969, Leyland and NBC each emerged with a 50% shareholding in the newly formed Bus Manufacturers (Holdings) Ltd, in which BCV was vested. This shared ownership survived until 1982 when Leyland bought out NBC; the works at Brislington closed the following year with production of the last model, the Olympian, transferred to Workington.

# BUT

British United Traction Ltd was a joint venture established by Leyland Motors and AEC for the construction of trolleybuses in 1946. Based at Kingston-upon-Thames, it initially occupied an erstwhile Leyland factory but later vehicles were manufactured at Southall, Stockport (in the former Crossley factory), and Watford. Trolleybuses were manufactured both for the domestic and export market but, as the trolleybus declined in popularity at home, production gradually fell and ceased completely in 1964 following the completion of an order for Wellington in New Zealand.

■ **ABOVE:** A British United Tractions trolleybus exported to the Netherlands.

17
BLACKBURN
434 BTE
REGENT

## Crossley

Crossley Motors Ltd was first registered in 1906 as the vehicle manufacturing arm of Crossley Brothers but the company did not start the manufacture of buses and trolleybuses in Manchester until after World War 1. The company's first bus model, the Eagle, was manufactured in 1928 although, as with the products of other commercial vehicle manufacturers, a number of Crossley lorries built for use by the military during World War 1 were subsequently fitted with bus bodies. The most successful model of bus produced by Crossley pre-1939 was the Mancunian, launched in 1933, which could be bodied either as a single- or double-deck vehicle. Crossley had a close relationship with Manchester Corporation – indeed only 22 out of 350 buses acquired by Manchester Corporation between 1930 and 1937 were not manufactured by Crossley – and so, when Manchester decided in 1935 to convert part of its tramway network to trolleybus operation, it was inevitable that it would turn to Crossley to build its new vehicles. In all, Crossley built 189 trolleybuses under its own name. In 1948 Crossley was acquired by AEC and the last Crossley-badged bus was manufactured in 1952. Following the takeover of the business by AEC, production of BUT trolleybus chasses was transferred to the ex-Crossley factory and almost 200 additional trolleybuses were built in Manchester; the last of these were completed for Glasgow in December 1958.

■ **LEFT:** An AEC Regent V, badged as produced by Crossley, supplied new to Darwen Corporation and later operated by Blackburn.

## Daimler

Based in Coventry, Daimler was one of Britain's first manufacturers of cars in the late 19th century, the manufacturer having acquired the UK rights to the patents claimed in Germany by Gottlieb Daimler. Significant bus production did not begin, however, until after World War 1. During the late 1920s, Daimler had a short-lived joint venture with AEC – the Associated Daimler Company – but this ended in 1929 and, from the 1930s, with models such as the COG5, available in both single- and double-deck variants, Daimler became an increasingly important manufacturer of buses, again primarily for the municipal sector. For a brief period from 1936 until after World War 2, Daimler also manufactured trolleybuses in a limited way. Becoming part of the Jaguar Group, Daimler was to become a subsidiary of British Motor Holdings in 1966 and subsequently part of the British Leyland Motor Corporation (BLMC). By the 1960s, as a result of the development of the Daimler Fleetline, one of the pioneering rear-entrance double-deck designs that was to become ultimately the standard London bus after production of the Routemaster ceased, Daimler was the second largest manufacturer of buses in Britain. However, after the company became part of the BLMC in 1968 the decision was made to transfer production away from the company's Coventry base in 1973 to the Leyland factory. Although production of the Fleetline continued until 1980, after about 1975 it was badged as a Leyland model.

■ **ABOVE:** A Daimler Fleetline bus.

■ **ABOVE:** Sir William Lyons, owner of Jaguar, Guy Motors, (buses on the right) and the Daimler Co, (buses and cars on the left), 1962.

## Guy

Founded in 1914 in Wolverhampton, Guy Motors was established by Sydney Guy, who had previously been Works Manager at the nearby Sunbeam factory. Initially production was of commercial vehicles, but after World War 1 production expanded to include buses and trolleybuses. In the mid-1920s, Guy Motors was the first to produce a three-axle bus; this model, which allowed for a much greater passenger capacity that helped make the bus more competitive against the tram, was also to be developed into the three-axle 'BTX' trolleybus. A two-axle version of the 'BTX', the 'BT' was launched in 1930. Although not one of the country's largest producers of buses, Guy Motors was selected as one of the few manufacturers permitted to produce new buses during World War 2. Two versions of the Guy Arab – the I and the II – were built between 1942 and 1945, with almost 3,000 constructed, most with so-called utility bodywork; the poor quality of the latter meant that many of these wartime vehicles were rebodied post-war in order to extend their working lives. Post-war, bus and trolleybus construction continued; the latter largely transferred to ex-Sunbeam Works following Guy Motors' acquisition of its local rival in 1948 until its closure in 1953. Trolleybus manufacture continued – under the Sunbeam name – until 1966 when the last vehicles to be produced were exported to Coimbra in Portugal. During the 1940s and 1950s, Guy continued to develop its conventional range of single- and double-deck models. In 1959, however, it launched the Wulfrunian. Although front-engined, the Wulfrunian was designed to allow a front-entrance body. In 1961 Guy Motors was taken over by Jaguar and bus production in Wolverhampton ceased in 1963 with the construction of the last Guy Arab IVs. The company itself passed to BLMC in 1968 with the factory finally closing in 1978.

# Leyland

The origins of Leyland Motors date back to the end of the 19th century when the Lancashire Steam Motor Company was established in the town of Leyland, just south of Preston. The company was renamed Leyland Motors in 1907 having started to manufacture petrol-engined lorries two years earlier. Bus production started in 1919 and, during the 1920s, with the success of the single-deck Lion, first produced in 1926, and the double-deck Titan, first produced the following year, was to become one of the dominant forces in British bus production by the outbreak of World War 2. Leyland was particularly successful in selling to the municipal market. The company continued to expand during the 1950s and 1960s, acquiring the interests of other businesses, such as Albion in 1951, Scammell in 1955 and Associated Commercial Vehicles (including AEC, Thornycroft and Park Royal) in 1962.

In 1968 Leyland merged with British Motor Holdings to form British Leyland Motor Corporation; this brought Daimler and Guy into the same ownership. With a 25% share of Bristol acquired in 1965, this meant that virtually all UK-controlled bus and coach manufacturing was held by a single company. However, the new BLMC proved unwieldy to manage and financially unsuccessful; it was nationalised in 1975 and the new business was split into four parts with the bus-manufacturing business forming part of Leyland Truck & Bus, later Leyland Bus. In 1987 the bus business, by then a pale shadow of the business inherited by the BLMC in 1968 with the closure of many of the factories, was sold to its management. The following year the business was sold once more, this time to Volvo. The sole remaining factory, that at Workington, closed in 1993 with all remaining work transferred to Volvo's factory at Irvine (which itself is now closed).

■ **ABOVE:** The first of the Leyland Olympic buses bound for Cuba, 1964.

■ **ABOVE:** Both the Derby and Wolverhampton trolleybuses in the foreground were products of Sunbeam with bodywork by Charles H. Roe.

## Sunbeam

The Sunbeam company was originally established as a trademark of John Marston Co Ltd of Wolverhampton in the late 19th century a manufacturer of bicycles and later cars, becoming the Sunbeam Motor Car Co Ltd in 1905. Following the production of aircraft during World War 1, the company diversified into the production of buses and trolleybuses in 1930 and 1932 respectively; production of the former was limited effectively to two double-deck models – the Pathan and DF2 – in limited numbers by the time that production ceased in 1948. In 1934 the bus and trolleybus part of the company was registered separately as Sunbeam Commercial Vehicles Ltd, which like the car business became a subsidiary of the Rootes Group. The Rootes Group also acquired another well-known trolleybus manufacturer, Karrier of Huddersfield, with production initially shifted to Luton, in 1935. Eventually Karrier production was moved from Huddersfield to the Moorfield Works, and it looked as if Sunbeam buses had a secure future. Both Karrier and Sunbeam continued to be marketed separately until after World War 2. In 1946 it was sold to Brockhouse, who in turn sold it to Guy Motors. Production at Moorfield Works continued until 1953 when it all moved to Guy's Works. The Sunbeam name survived until the 1960s, producing the last new trolleybuses manufactured for the British market – a batch of MF2Bs produced for Bournemouth in 1963 – until production ceased in 1966.

## Thornycroft

Dating originally from the late 19th century, Thornycroft moved from Chiswick, where it had been established, to Basingstoke in 1898. The company produced a steam-powered bus for London in 1902 and this was followed by two more for the Belfast & Northern Counties Railway in Ireland (B&NCR). The B&NCR was also the purchaser of the company's first petrol-engined charabancs in 1905. A small-scale producer of buses at this time, Thornycroft was best known as a lorry manufacturer, although a number of these – such as three built for the Great North of Scotland Railway in 1915/16 – were bodied as buses. After World War 1 a large number of ex-military lorries were rebuilt as buses. The first dedicated bus chassis, the A1, appeared in 1924 with notable customers including the Great Western Railway. The A1 was followed by the A2 and by the Lightning in 1927. Much of the company's production during the late 1920s was exported but this declined along with the world economy in the early 1930s. In 1931 the Daring double-deck and Cygnet single-deck models were launched and the company also produced its own diesel engine in 1934. The last double-deck buses supplied pre-war went to Southampton Corporation in 1937. Post-war the bulk of the company's bus production was based upon the HF Nippy lorry, which was supplied up until 1950 although a limited number of true bus chasses were built in the late 1940s. Thornycroft was taken over by AEC in 1961 by which date bus production had long ceased.

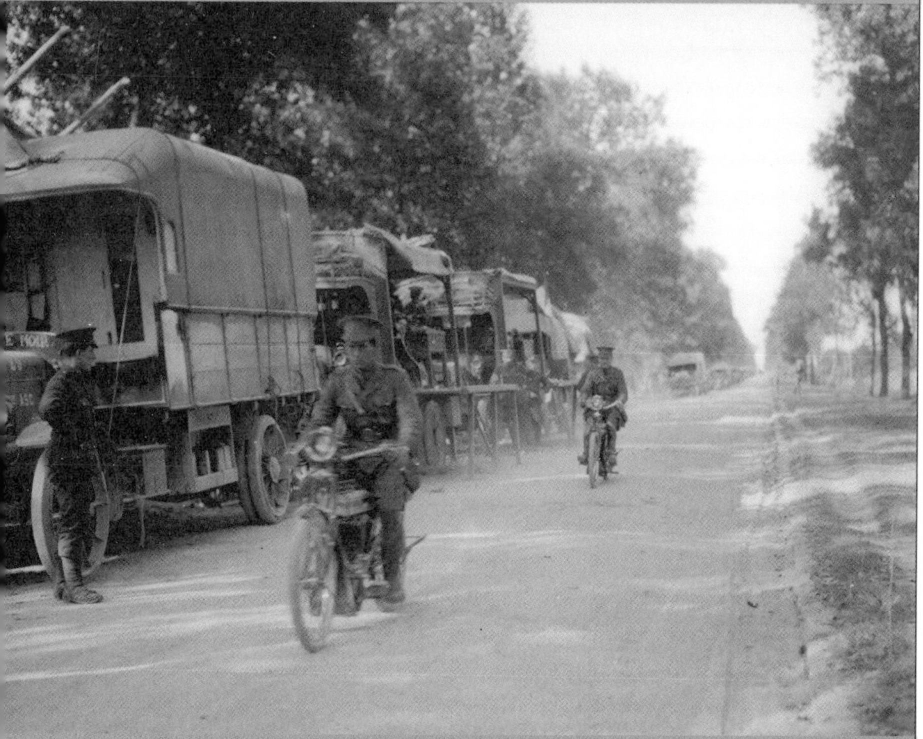

■ **ABOVE:** Thornycroft lorries used during World War 1, 1914.

■ **ABOVE:** A single-deck tramcar in 1901 about to travel from Central Station in Newcastle to Osborne Road.

## Tram Builders

Although there were a number of bus operators – such as London General (which later became AEC), Bristol Tramways & Carriage Co (Bristol) and Midland Red (which continued to produce its own vehicles as part of the BET Group until the 1960s) – that built there own buses, the vast majority of buses built were by outside contractors. With trams, however, many of the operators, even relatively small-scale systems, regularly built or rebuilt their own tramcars, sourcing parts, for example the trucks and the electrical equipment, from outside contractors. Municipal fleets including Blackpool, Bradford, Dundee, Edinburgh, Glasgow, Leeds, Liverpool and Sheffield, all had a significant number of trams built in their own workshops. For smaller manufacturers, however, there were a number of manufacturers who could supply trams. These included Starbuck (Birkenhead; originally established in 1862 and producing 3,000 trams for the home and export market between then and closure in 1913), G. F. Milnes & Co (Shropshire), Dick Kerr (of Kilmarnock and Preston, which later became part of English Electric), Hurst Nelson (Motherwell) and Brush (Loughborough).

# The Classic Buses

## Leyland Titan

The first of Leyland's family of Leyland Titans, the TD1, was launched in 1927, two years before the first of the AEC Regent types. When it first appeared, the model was claimed to be the most modern double-deck design produced. Initially fitted with a Leyland petrol engine, the bus was largely supplied with bodywork also manufactured by Leyland, although some operators selected bodywork from elsewhere. By the time that production of the TD1 ceased in 1932 some 2,300 had been built, with operators including Bolton Corporation, Warrington Corporation, Southdown and Southern National. The TD1 was the first of a family of Leyland front-engined designs that were to continue in production through to the PD3 in 1969. Leyland double-deck designs were to be found in the fleets of most operators, including London Transport, which acquired 1,631 PD2/7RTs between 1948 and 1954 (the 'RTL'-type). A handful of the original TD1 models survive in preservation.

■ **ABOVE:** Mechanic checking the engine of a Leyland bus in 1957.

■ **ABOVE:** A 1957 AEC Regent III/Park Royal of Reading Corporation.

## AEC Regent III

First manufactured in 1947, the Regent III was AEC's double-deck model for sale outside the London area. In all, more than 5,930 of the type were built between then and 1957 with 76 being supplied to London Transport (the 'RLH' type) with examples finding their way to many municipal and company operators nationwide. The London version (the 'RT' type) was first manufactured in 1946 and was a modified version of the model first introduced in 1939 and was designated the Regent IIIRT. The 'RT' was the standard double-deck design supplied to London Transport between 1946 and 1954 when production ceased; in all, London Transport received 4,674 post-war 'RT'-type vehicles, with the last surviving in service until 1979. Apart from London Transport, there was only one customer from new for the IIIRT model; this was St Helens Corporation, although a considerable number of ex-London Transport vehicles were to see service elsewhere when sold into the second-hand market. A number of municipal operators – such as Dundee – acquired ex-LT IIIRTs for use as tramway replacement vehicles. Outside London, the majority of AEC Regent IIIs had been withdrawn by the early 1970s, but a significant number of both the Regent III and IIIRT types survive in preservation.

# Karrier/Sunbeam W4

Produced originally in 1942 to Ministry of Supply specifications, the Karrier/Sunbeam W4 – it was marketed under both names although the former was more common – was one of the most important trolleybus types to be constructed in Britain and the only model produced in significant quantities during World War 2. The first of the model was supplied to Darlington and, by the time production ceased in the late 1940s, almost 470 of the model had been built. Although the majority were fitted with double-deck bodies, a small number delivered to Darlington Corporation and Mexborough & Swinton, were originally single-deckers. The longevity of many trolleybus chasses ensured that many of the vehicles were rebodied during their careers and a number were still in service with Bradford Corporation when almost 30 years old in March 1972, as the final trolleybus network in the country was converted to bus operation. Almost 20 of the type survive in preservation.

■ **RIGHT:** Karrier W trolleybus exhibit at Bradford Industrial Museum.

7
THORNTON
737
DKY 737

Museum of British Road Transport
Coventry
333

## Daimler CV Series

After the cessation of hostilities in 1945, Daimler introduced a new range of double- and single-deck models in 1946 and 1947 respectively. A range of engines was offered. For the double-deck designs, the engine variants were the Gardner 5LW (known as the CVG5), the Gardner 6LW (the CVG6), the Daimler CD6 (the CVD6) and an AEC 7.7 litre engine (the CVA6); the last was relatively short-lived and the model was to continue in production until 1965. There were two variants for the single-deck market – the CVG5 and the CVD6 – although the former was only available until 1949 and the latter until 1955. The Daimler/Gardner combination of double-deck design was popular with many municipalities, with examples being found in many towns and cities across the UK – including Birmingham, Bradford, Coventry, Derby, Dundee, Edinburgh, Exeter, Manchester, Salford and West Bromwich – and in the export trade where a significant number found their way to Hong Kong. The last of the CVG6 models were withdrawn in the early 1980s and a number have survived into preservation.

■ **LEFT:** Coventry Motor Museum agreed to let the Girl Guides clean a 1963 Daimler bus for charity.

## Bristol Lodekka

One of the most intractable problems with double-deck design was to try and ensure that it was possible to achieve sensible headroom on both decks; historically, the height of the chassis meant that to achieve this headroom the bus bodies were made higher – hence 'highbridge' bus designs – which caused problems when operating in areas with low bridges and other restrictions. If a lower body was required – the so-called 'lowbridge' design – this could only be achieved through a rearrangement of the upper deck and the inclusion of a sunken passageway. The Bristol Lodekka was a radical solution to the problem in that it provided a lower chassis that enabled two full-height decks to be provided within the height of a conventional 'lowbridge' design. The first prototype of this radical design emerged from Brislington in 1949 with a second coming the following year. Production of the Lodekka, as the model was known, commenced in 1953 and over 5,200 examples of the design were built before production ceased in 1968. Of these, all were provided with Eastern Coach Works' bodies and with the vast majority going to Tilling Group operators. A small number were also supplied to the Scottish Bus Group. The original model featured a rear platform but after 1961 all were supplied with front-entrance bodies. As a result of restrictions placed on the supply of Bristol models outside the Tilling Group, production of the Lodekka was licensed to Dennis of Guildford and marketed under the name of Loline. Operation of the Lodekka model largely ceased in the early 1980s but examples of both the rear- and front-entrance types survive in preservation.

■ **ABOVE:** Bristol Lodekka LD6B/ECW.

229
FARNBOROUGH
10
LIVERPOOL STREET

## AEC Routemaster

Arguably now the most familiar type of bus ever built in the British Isles and instantly recognisable as a symbol of London, the first Routemaster emerged as a prototype from AEC's Southall factory in 1954. The design brief was to produce a vehicle that was lighter (hence more fuel efficient), easier to operate and to be maintained by the existing maintenance practices at the recently opened Aldenham Works. The resulting production vehicle could carry 64 seated passengers despite weighing three-quarters of a ton less than the previous RT that could carry 56 seated passengers. It was an innovative design compared with previous buses, and used lightweight aluminium and techniques developed in aircraft production during World War 2. As well as a novel weight-saving integral design, the Routemaster also introduced (for the first time on a bus) independent front suspension, power steering, a fully automatic gearbox and power-hydraulic braking. The Routemaster design was a departure from the traditional chassis/body construction method. With London Transport being the primary customer, the option to use different bodybuilders was less important. The design was one of the first 'integral' buses, with the bus being a combination of an 'A' steel sub-frame (including engine, steering and front suspension), and a rear 'B' steel sub-frame (carrying rear axle and suspension), connected by the aluminium body. The gearbox was mounted on the underside of the body structure with shafts linking the engine to the back axle.

Production of the type in large numbers commenced in 1958 with the aim of using the Routemaster to replace London's trolleybus network. Manufacture continued until 1968 and, apart from London Transport, small numbers were also supplied to British

■ **ABOVE:** Row of Routemaster buses at Chiswick bus garage, 1962.

European Airways and to Northern General. In all 2,876 Routemasters were built, although there were some variations. The standard Routemaster was designated 'RM' in London; these were 27ft 6in (8.4m) in length. The 30ft (9m) version was designated 'RML'. The 'RMC' was a coach version produced for Green Line services and the 'RCL' was a 30ft-long version of the 'RMC'. The 'RMF' and 'RMA' types were front-entrance models built for BEA and Northern General with one – RMF 1254 – originally being built for London Transport. There was also a single prototype – FRM 1 – as a rear-engined model in 1966.

From the late 1970s, with the pressure to convert routes to OPO, the number of Routemasters in London gradually declined, although many were to find a second life outside London when they were pressed into service by operators seeking a competitive edge in the era of deregulation. Thus it became possible to see Routemasters in operation in places as far apart as Southend, Blackpool and Perth. However, the type was to see a revival in London from the early 1990s when many of those that had survived underwent refurbishment and some sold examples were later reacquired for restoration to service. In 2004, it was announced that, for a variety of reasons, the Routemaster was to be phased out of service and the last scheduled route to operate the Routemaster – the 159 – was converted to alternative buses on 9 December 2005, bringing to an end 50 years of service.

This is, however, not quite the end of the story as a limited number of Routemasters continue to ply their trade on two heritage routes in central London and countless others survive in preservation.

## Daimler Fleetline

The Daimler Fleetline was the second type of rear-engined double-deck bus to be launched into the British market, in 1960, following on from the Leyland Atlantean that had been first produced in 1958. The model was destined to be the last double-deck type produced by Daimler, being manufactured in Coventry until 1973, when the Daimler factory closed, and then by Leyland at Farington until production ceased in 1980. For the last five years of production it was badged as a Leyland. During the 1960s manufacturers continued to produce both front- and rear-engined buses as the market was there for both; however, from 1968 the New Bus Grant was only available for the purchase of rear-engined buses and so the market for front-engined buses rapidly disappeared. The Fleetline, the Atlantean and Bristol's VR represented effectively the only double-deck models available and so all three sold in large numbers during the late 1960s and 1970s until replaced by the Olympian. The single largest customer for the Fleetline was London Transport, which acquired 2,646 of the marque, designating them either as 'DM' or 'DMS'. Planned to be the standard London bus following on from the Routemaster the Fleetline, despite surviving in service in London until 1993, was not as successful as its rear-entrance predecessor. Outside London, there were significant fleets amongst the Passenger Transport Executives, with West Midlands operating more than 1,000 of the type and Greater Manchester more than 500. Apart from the domestic market, a significant number of Fleetlines were also exported, with many being sold to operators in Hong Kong. One curious fact is that both the original prototype and the last to be built were both destroyed in fires, the latter shortly after it was preserved.

■ **ABOVE:** Metrobus Routemaster RML and a London Transport Park Royal bodied Daimler Fleetline passing each other.

■ **ABOVE:** Citybus 2565 (BXI 2565), a Bristol RE/Alexander (Belfast) X Type.

## Bristol RE

Considered to be the most successful of the first generation of rear-engined single-deck bus designs, the Bristol RE was first produced at Brislington in 1962. As with other Bristol-built buses, the supplies of the RE were initially limited to subsidiaries of the nationalised Transport Holding Company and it was only after the sale of a share in the business to Leyland that the market for the type was expanded. Following this the model was sold to non-Tilling Group companies. The majority of those vehicles supplied were bodied by ECW in Lowestoft. Designed primarily for stage carriage services, a number were also constructed for express coach service. Production of the RE largely ceased in 1976, following the launch of the Leyland National – the joint venture between Leyland and NBC – but production continued until 1982 largely for the supply of vehicles to Ulsterbus and Citybus in Northern Ireland and for the export market. Operation of the RE had largely ceased by the late 1990s although a number survive in preservation.

■ **ABOVE RIGHT:** In Ryde depot, Isle of Wight, 1979.

## Leyland National

Following the creation of the National Bus Company the newly-nationalised bus operator sought a standard single-deck design to replace models such as the Bristol RE, the AEC Swift and the Leyland Panther. In a joint venture with British Leyland, the Leyland National was the result, with manufacture concentrated at a brand-new factory opened at Workington in Cumbria. The Leyland National was built with integral, modular construction and a rear engine. All components were designed for ease of construction and replacement. Until 1978, it was always built with a distinctive roof-mounted pod at the rear, housing the heating equipment, which consequently blew warm air out at roof level. At first the pod was almost the length of a bay and appeared to be designed to give a transatlantic feel. In 1974 a new shorter version of the roof pod was introduced. The Leyland National was available in two lengths, 33ft 8in (10.3m) and 37ft 1in (11.3m). It was easy to spot the shorter one because of its squarer windows. The National 2 was introduced in 1979. It differed from its predecessor mainly by having a front-mounted radiator and a choice of engines. Production of the Leyland National ceased in 1985, by which stage more than 7,000 of the type had been built. It was replaced by the Leyland Lynx, which was built between 1984 and 1992. By that date large numbers had been supplied to constituent companies of the NBC along with a number of non-NBC operators. These included the Scottish Bus Group, London Transport (where it was designated the 'LN'-type) and the export market. Although some of the Leyland Nationals underwent a mid-life refurbishment, the last surviving vehicles were taken out of service towards the end of the first decade of the 21st century. A number can, however, still be seen in preservation.

224 WORKS SERVICE
6169
6169
CKB 166X

## Leyland Olympian

Although Leyland was manufacturing the integral Leyland Titan in large numbers for London Transport, a significant demand remained for non-integral double-deck models from operators outside the Metropolis and the result was the Bristol Olympian. First manufactured at the erstwhile Bristol factory at Brislington, until its closure in 1983, and at Farington in Lancashire, production of the Olympian was eventually concentrated on the ex-Leyland National factory at Workington. In 1988 Leyland Bus was acquired by Volvo although production of the Olympian continued at Workington until 1993 when the factory closed. Production was then transferred to the Volvo factory at Irvine, where it continued to be manufactured as the Volvo Olympian until the model was withdrawn in 2000. The Olympian proved popular in the domestic market with significant numbers being sold to London Transport, to the various Passenger Transport Executives, to many of the surviving municipal operators, to subsidiaries of the National Bus Company prior to privatisation and to Hong Kong and Singapore. For the export market, Leyland designed a longer three-axle version. A significant number of the later Olympians still remain in service.

7
Alum Ba
We Accept Euro Notes
710
SOUTHERN
VECTIS
the island's buses
TIL 6710

■ **ABOVE:** Cliff Richard prepares for his role in *Summer Holiday* at the Chiswick driving school.

# Buses and Trams in Popular Culture

Although there are not many films and television programmes that feature public transport in anything other than an incidental role, there are a few that do use buses or trams in a central role. Of these, the most famous is undoubtedly Cliff Richards' musical *Summer Holiday*, which was originally released in 1963 and directed by Peter Yates. Although often cited as a Routemaster, the type of double-deck bus actually featured was an earlier design of London Transport bus – the RT – which is recorded on a journey from London to Athens.

Starring the late Reg Varney, the sitcom *On the Buses* ran on British commercial television for 74 episodes between 1969 and 1973. The series featured buses operated by two fictional bus operators: the green-liveried Luxton & District and the red-liveried Town & District. The majority of the vehicles were Bristols supplied by Eastern National. There were three spin-off films produced: *On the Buses* (1971), *Mutiny on the Buses* (1972) and *Holiday on the Buses* (1973).

■ **ABOVE RIGHT:** Bob Grant actor from TV series *On the Buses* marries Kim Benwell.

Buses also feature in two cameo roles of note. In Roger Moore's first appearance as James Bond in *Live and Let Die*, directed by Guy Hamilton and released in 1973, the British agent at one stage makes good his escape in an ex-London Transport RT that eventually sheds its top deck passing under a low bridge. If losing a deck was one attribute of the RT, in *Harry Potter and the Prisoner of Azkaban*, the third in the series and directed by Alfonso Cuarón, a triple-deck version of the type makes a prominent appearance.

Trams and trolleybuses have appeared in a number of documentary films. Apart from a large number produced primarily for the enthusiast market, a number of films at a more general audience were also shot. These include *The Elephant Will Never Forget*, produced by British Transport Films to mark the final withdrawal of London's trams in 1952, and 9 *Dalmuir West*, produced by Kevin Brownlow to commemorate the demise of trams in Glasgow a decade later. Many

■ **ABOVE:** The launch of *Harry Potter and the Prisoner of Azkaban*.

of the short films shot by Mitchell and Kenyon, now available through the British Film Institute, also record scenes with tram interest taken in the years prior to the outbreak of World War 1.

In terms of memorabilia, apart from the preserved vehicles themselves, there is much to interest the potential collector. Historic postcards offer one route to acquire photographs of old vehicles; many, moreover, have the advantage of showing the bus or tram in the street and thus help to put the vehicle into its historical context. More specifically it is possible to build collections of historic tram and bus tickets – there's even a society (The Transport Ticket Society) – for those interested in the subject. Other items of public transport interest that can be acquired are the old-fashioned bus stops, ticket machines and uniforms.

For those interested in seeing historic trams preserved or in operation there are a number of museums that operate trams.

■ **ABOVE LEFT:** Roger Moore with his wife at the Premiere of *Live and Let Die*, 1973.

■ **ABOVE RIGHT:** London Transport bus drivers collecting for charity in their uniforms during World War 2.

The National Tramway Museum at Crich – known as the Crich Tramway Village – is situated in Derbyshire and houses one of the largest collections of tramcars in the world. Examples of house, steam and electric trams are displayed and it is possible to ride on many of the restored electric trams. Three other sites in England – the Black Country Museum near Dudley, the East Anglian Transport Museum near Lowestoft and the Heaton Park Tramway near Manchester – also have operational electric tramways. In Scotland, the Summerlee Heritage Park near Coatbridge also has a short operational tramway. Static tramcars are preserved in a number

■ **ABOVE:** London tram number 1858 moved to the East Anglian Transport Museum at Lowestoft.

of museums nationwide, including the London Transport Museum in Covent Garden and at the new Glasgow Museum of Transport, which is scheduled to open in 2011.

There is an operational trolleybus museum at Sandtoft, near Doncaster, and both the Black Country and East Anglian Transport museums also regularly operate trolleybuses. Static examples can be found on display elsewhere, including the Bradford Industrial Museum at Moorside Mills and the London Transport Museum.

There are numerous collections of buses displayed nationwide. Significant collections can be found at Aston

■ **ABOVE:** Lenny Henry at the London Transport Museum.

Manor Road Transport Museum (near Birmingham), the Keighley Bus Museum (near Bradford), the Scottish Vintage Bus Museum (Lathalmond), the Cobham Bus Museum (Cobham), Manchester Museum of Transport (Manchester), Wythall Transport Museum (Wythall), Oxford Bus Museum (Long Hanborough) and the Isle of Wight Bus & Coach Museum (Newport, Isle of Wight) amongst many others. Many of these have specials events and regular open days. Information about events and other museums can be found in the pages of specialist magazines such as *Buses* and *Bus & Coach Preservation*, both of which are published monthly.

■ **ABOVE:** Buses in the Manchester Transport Museum, all in their original liveries.